# Highlights

# TONGUE TWISTERS!

## The TRICKIEST TWISTIEST JOKE BOOK EVER!

HA HA HA
HA HA

Highlights Press
Honesdale, Pennsylvania

Contributing Illustrators: Emily Balsley, Eric Barclay, Paula Becker, Jim Bradshaw, Iryna Bodnaruk, Anja Boretzki, Jenny Campbell, C.B. Canga, Dave Clegg, Josh Cleland, Laura Ferraro Close, Daryll Collins, David Coulson, Stacy Curtis, Mike Dammer, Mike DeSantis, Jack Desrocher, Joey Ellis, Carolina Farias, Martin Filchock, Keith Frawley, Stephen Gilpin, Patrick Girouard, Valeri Gorbachev, Susan T. Hall, David Helton, Jimmy Holder, Paul Hoppe, Kelly Kennedy, Greg Kletsel, Dave Klug, James Kochalka, Gary Lacoste, Pat Lewis, Mike Lowery, Steve Mack, Lyn Martin, Erin Mauterer, Rob McClurkan, Katie McDee, Howard McWilliam, Paul Montgomery, Julissa Mora, Mike Moran, Mitch Mortimer, Wally Neibart, Neil Numberman, Jim Paillot, Tamara Petrosino, Rich Powell, Kevin Rechin, Rico Schacherl, Christine Schneider, Erica Sirotich, Jackie Stafford, Gary Swift, Vin Vogel, Pete Whitehead, Daniel Wiseman, Ron Zalme, Kevin Zimmer

For information about permission to reprint selections from this book, please contact permissions@highlights.com.

Published by Highlights Press
815 Church Street
Honesdale, Pennsylvania 18431

ISBN: 978-1-64472-865-9
Library of Congress Control Number: 2022933907

Manufactured in Robbinsville, NJ, USA
Mfg. 06/2022

First edition
Visit our website at Highlights.com.

10 9 8 7 6 5 4 3 2 1

# Contents

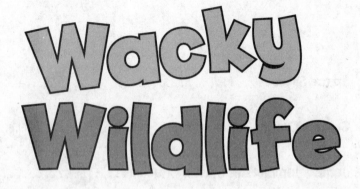

Wacky Wildlife

Elephants led the elaborate antics.

Are orangutans always orange?

In the bus's back sat snacking yaks.

9

**An ape ate eighteen apples in April.**

Don't double-dare daring deer!

A band of baffling, bumbling baboons.

Ferrets dress in festive vests.

**Lazing lions gaze at gazelles.**

Chuck Chipmunk
chewed chestnuts.

**Zed is a zebra who sells snazzy zippers.**

The white-whiskered, weary,
wet walrus went west.

**Two tired toads tied twine.**

Will a gorilla grill a
burger?

A big black bug bit a big black bear.

Gary Giraffe gave Greta Gazelle a grape.

Squirrels quarrel quietly.

**Charming chimps chomp chips.**

Chilly cheetahs chow
on chewy cherries.

**Reading frogs favor fables.**

Hal and Hilly Hippo
hollered hello.

**If goose goes to *geese*, do two
moose make *meese*?**

Juggling jaguars jumped
on the jungle gym.

**Apes ate green grapes.**

Sue's new gnu knew shoes!

**Mama Llama's pajama drama.**

Let the restless lemurs wrestle.

**Black bears baked braided bread.**

Twelve tigers twirled
twelve twigs.

**So many monkeys smile sneakily.**

Grumpy grizzlies growl
gruffly.

**Moose
munches
as Monkey
amuses
Mouse.**

Yellow yaks wear speckled slacks.

Intelligent elephants are excellent smellers.

White rhinos write witty rhymes.

Britt brought both bears.

Shocked chimps chided
sleeping sheep.

**Brown bears barely notice
nosy neighbors.**

Lava llama momma.

Groggy
gophers
goggle at
goofier
golfers.

**Five funky monkeys
munching five
fried munchies.**

An ape ate an apple appetizer.

Cheeky chipmunks in
chimneys chase each other.

The more Maura mimes monkeys, the less Lester likes lemurs.

Kevin cared for cave critters.

**Yawning yaks sat stacking black hats.**

Rare rhinos rolled real red wagons.

**If you go for a gopher, a gopher will go for a gopher hole.**

Aardvarks are oddly awkward.

**Many monkeys made maracas.**

Cheating cheetahs chew chocolates.

**The other otter uttered eighty idioms.**

Daring deer don't dawdle.

A tiny tiger tied a tie
tighter to tidy his tiny tail.

Many moose mash much mush.

Wally Walrus washed his
whiskers.

A fox in socks balances
a box on rocks.

**Silently, Sheila slinks.**

Ty tries to tame the tiger.

A happy hippopotamus
must hippety-hop.

Walruses waved from race cars.

**Busy bison buy sunny businesses.**

A rafting giraffe rafts
the rapids rapidly.

**Camels making mascots' masks.**

Four freckled frogs
fried French flies.

**Wolves wove woolly scarves.**

"Plums, please!"
pandas pleaded.

A skunk sunk the dunk
from a junk trunk.

**Who can anger a kangaroo?**

Raccoons raise a
raucous racket.

**Hedgehogs dodge logs.**

**Squirrel squished squash.**

Suppose a possum possibly assumes some poses.

**The shy, sleepy groundhog was shocked to see his shadow.**

When a weasel sneezes, she wheezes.

**A lynx likes linking things.**

Antelopes can't elope with cantaloupes.

# Bird Bloopers

**Pheasants present pleasant presents.**

**Some swans swim sideways.**

Ollie Owl only wears
orange overalls.

Egrets grow greatly.

Fawn feeds fish to feathered friends.

Is an eagle more regal than a seagull?

The quail quailed at the quick quiz.

**Big birds buy buns.**

Cardinals chew
hard caramels.

Squirming swans squabble
with squawking quails.

A pelican can pile
a bunch in its pouch.

**A rude roadrunner ran rather rapidly.**

Ravenous ravens arrived at the ravine.

**Draw drowsy ducks and drakes.**

A leaf swirls; a swallow flies.

**Eight eagles equal eight.**

The bluebird blinks
at the blackbird.

**Flocks fly from fallen trees.**

A squawking hawk stalks
an awkward auk.

Famous
flamingos
dance the
flamenco!

A red bird braided a bramble.

Free falcons flee the forest.

Gray geese graze
in the green grass.

Condors wonder where to wander.

**Prank-playing pigeons.**

Six silky swans swarm
the sticky swamp.

**Peacocks peep past pretty parrots.**

The eager egret eagerly
eyes the feeble beetle.

**Fidgety finches switch fences.**

A dove dove into
a lovely cove.

**Small quail smile widely.**

A goose goes loose
in the caboose!

**Three thrushes rushed through
the brush.**

Burt's bird brought
bread to bed.

Crows rose, crazily cackling.

An ostrich stood on
a strange ridge.

Rory saw an ornery oriole.

Great Grandma Gertie's
geese giggle.

The bird-watcher watched the bird watch the bird-watcher.

**A sparrow cowers under a borrowed wheelbarrow.**

Elusive emus amuse easily.

**Would woodpeckers peck wood if wood would peck back?**

The vulgar vulture wore velour.

Five flinching finches
find feathers.

Do sparrows follow swallows?

Herons hurry home.

**Picnicking peacocks
picked polka dots.**

**Birds bathe in warm, wet water.**

Hummingbirds happily hum.

Falcons flinched
while finches flew.

Do hurrying hawks hike or walk?

**Birds borrow brown bread.**

Wrens run when rare
herons are here.

**Chickadees cheekily chuckled.**

Ruby the running roadrunner
ran on a rocky road.

**Larks like chocolate licorice.**

Grumpy grouse grouse
about the bouncy house.

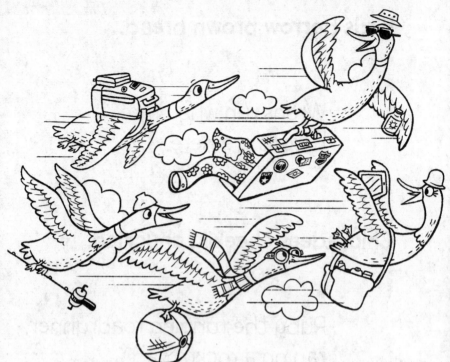

A gaggle of giddy geese goes by.

Pudgy penguins picked pretty posies.

Egrets regret forgetting
baguettes.

**My feathered friend Fred.**

Six sleek swans swam
swiftly southward.

**Warblers warned
burger burglars.**

Could a cuckoo
cook a cookie?

**In the kitchen, pigeons
pitch in.**

Farm Fun

**Rapid rabbits ran rampant.**

**Great gray goats.**

Pete Brigg's pink pig's
big pig's pigpen.

Rowdy roosters ramble
around the barnyard.

The white wheelbarrow
was wacky and wild.

**Sheep should sleep in a shed.**

One rabbit ran;
one rabbit won.

**Corey chooses corn carefully.**

Howie knows how
to hoe whole rows.

**Seven sneaky scarecrows.**

Poppy passes pretty
ponies on the path.

Roy Goat
rows a
toy boat.

**A frog and a pig jog
on a long log.**

If a rooster crows,
does a crow rooster?

**Never cram a lamb
and a ram in a van.**

Shar and Chad
share the orchard.

## High silo or low silo?

Swine swill from
the rough trough.

## Stu strews stray straw.

Prop crops properly
with strong stakes.

The flustered flock scattered in a flash.

**Sound asleep like sheep.**

**Hungry horses hunt for hay.**

Twelve turkeys twirled twine on a tractor.

**Waddling wild ducks dawdle.**

**Cooper keeps the coop cooler.**

Cheery chicks chirp,
"Cheep-cheep!"

**Farmer Hayes hauls hay all day.**

In May, merry Mary sheared
sixty silly sheep.

**Steer clear of the restless steer!**

One must milk many milk
cows daily at the dairy.

**Eight appealing apples sated the Appaloosa's appetite.**

**Mighty mustang stallions must impress mustang mares.**

Cheeping chicks
peeped sleepily.

**Sweep swiftly while swine sleep.**

Roosters rouse resters
from their roosts.

**Ravenous rabbits roasted radishes.**

Sam shaved seven
shy sheep.

**Greedy goats pluck grapes.**

Cows would crouch on couches if they could.

She shouldn't have shorn the sheep so short.

Harvey harvests heavy veggies.

**A mole rode a mile on a mule.**

Who knew the ewe was new?

**Coloring colorful cats is complicated when counting crazy cows.**

**Irina arranges oranges on her ranch.**

**Cow couldn't count without a calculator.**

Of course his horse is off course.

Are you sure our shaggy sheep were shorn?

Six sassy sheep shop sassily.

**Otis boasts the best oats.**

Maddie mowed the meadow immediately.

**Felicia fled the fly-filled field.**

Pass the batch of peach baskets!

**Coddle cuddly cattle.**

Pretty pintos and painted ponies prance around the paddock.

Evelyn lays exactly
eleven eggs.

A sloppy hog slumps on a
soggy stump.

Shepherds schlepping
spoiled sheep.

# Find five fillies frolicking.

Bernard barred bears
from his barnyard.

## Sam's lamb samples brambles.

Ian installs his tall stallions
in their stalls.

Can a cow chef cook chewy cookies?

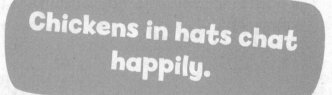

Chickens in hats chat happily.

Pasha pushed past the pastor's pasture.

Six silly sheep sleep soundly.

**Baby bunnies babble amiably.**

Hungry horses hoard
heaps of hay.

**Waddling wild ducks dawdle.**

Al's farmer father
farms alfalfa.

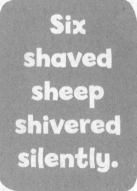

**Six
shaved
sheep
shivered
silently.**

Punny Pets

## Donald's dogs dug deep.

**Listen! Blissful kittens.**

Perry's parrot is partial to pears.

**Tiny turtles tried on tutus.**

Terry terrifies a furrier terrier.

Catch a kitten in a kitchen
caught in cotton candy.

Tara keeps a parakeet.

**Liza's lizard lies lazily.**

Never give a skinny
fig to a guinea pig.

**Fifty kiddies cuddle fifty kitties.**

Goldie's goldfish play
Go Fish gladly.

**Fletcher fetches five stiff sticks.**

Bonnie's bunny nibbles
nubby hay.

Every ferret feels very furry.

Suds shocked Spot.

**Iris's Irish setter wears stylish sweaters.**

Gilbert gurgles at the glowing goldfish.

Sal and Amanda share
a salamander.

Don't trouble timid turtles.

Kelly cuddled her calico cat.

Posey's dog does yoga poses.

**Geri's gerbil bakes gingerbread.**

Ten tiny turtles sitting in a tiny tin tub turned tan.

Puppies playfully prance with pink and purple pigs.

# The feline feasted fast on fat fish.

A dog with decorations from Denmark.

## Fetch, Filch, fetch!

Pilar caught a caterpillar on her cat pillow.

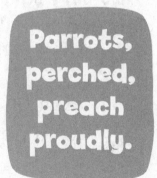

**Parrots, perched, preach proudly.**

If Stu chews shoes, should Stu choose which shoes he chews?

Tia's tiny turtle tastes a little lettuce.

Kaitlyn caught her kitten sniffing muffins.

Sam disturbs his sister's hamster.

**Bailey borrowed Barkley's bone.**

Black dachshunds
shun the hot sun.

**Carla clipped the cat's claws.**

The drowsy schnauzer
snores and dozes.

Nary a
canary
can carry
a tune.

 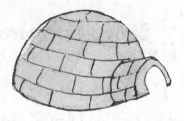

**Iggy's iguana lives in an igloo.**

Rex wrecks Rick's shoes.

Tabitha's tabby is terribly crabby.

Dogs dig deep ditches.

**Katniss catnaps near her catnip.**

Dora adores her
Labrador, Laura!

**Katrina's cat chomped kibble.**

Chester chose a
squeaky chew toy.

**Careless cats clawed and crawled.**

Colleen's collie collects collars.

**Big dogs dig bones.**

"Must pass the mustard to my mutt," my mother muttered.

The cat attacked a stack of snacks.

Rover retrieves Trevor's Frisbee.

# Lost cat's trophy? A catastrophe!

Doug dogged his
dog Dawg doggedly.

## Five flying felines fled fleas.

Drew's dog Denny
got drenched.

Kate's
cat can't
skate.

**Which leash is least long?**

Dogs drink, dance, dig,
and drum doors.

Frieda's friend Frank
found Fido first.

# Which Chihuahua chews what?

Pappy's puppy lapped
up a purple pop.

**Daniel's spaniel can heel dandily.**

The beagle brought
bagels for breakfast.

Does Doogie's poodle do the doggy paddle?

Nifty kitten knitting!

The dainty dog drooled and dillydallied.

Pippa's puppy pops up at puppets.

# Doggone dog's gone!

Baxter the boxer backs down the back stairs.

**Spot sports a short leash.**

Fleas tease these Siamese kitties.

**Dot sports spots as Spot slurps pots.**

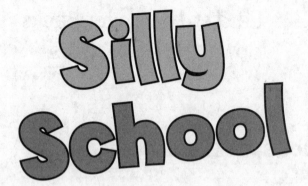

Silly School

**Loopy llamas love learning letters.**

**Benny Betta buys a book.**

Ten tacky tacks in
a tacky tack tin.

**Liquid glue.**

**Wesley sings as Leslie swings.**

The class clock clicked clearly.

Hillie's hopscotch had
Hannah hopping happily.

Tim taught Tom to tell a tale.

**Priscilla packs purple pencils.**

Brook's brown book is bigger
than Blake's black book.

**Addison adds several sevens.**

Helwig helped Homer
with homework.

**Ernest yearns to learn in earnest.**

Charlie chooses chalk;
Prim prefers pencils.

**Stan staples Peter's papers.**

Theo drew three triangles.

One black backpack is brown.
One brown backpack is black.

Celia slurped spiced cider.

**All our *R*'s are ours for hours.**

Ronald and Raymond
read riddles.

**My marker makes messes.**

Mark marks Brooke's
books with bookmarks.

**Ed had edited it.**

Surely Shirley should
start to study soon.

**Tex took the textbooks.**

Gidget goes gaga over digits.

Rodney wrote a word with rhythm.

Greg gained great grades in geography.

**Sarah slid down several slides.**

Britta brought a
bright blue beret.

**Bring your books brookside.**

Cactus? Practice?
I pick practice.

Scott
skates to
school.

Sarah and Sam sang seven silly songs at school.

Ed aided Addy in adding to eighty.

Commas cause pauses after clauses.

# Justin just jots notes jauntily.

Silly Sally snoozes
on the seesaw.

## Reese's recess rocked.

Lucy lurches with
her lunch tray.

**Dish up double
dips of spuds.**

**Charlie and Cheryl cheer shrilly.**

**Story time: a timeless storytelling time.**

Simple subtraction simply stumps Steven.

The blue glue grew green goo.

Drew draws dreadfully dreary drawings.

**Mark makes marker marks.**

Brock's books break Blake's backpack.

**Silly Sally always slides sideways.**

Alfie fit but a bit of the alphabet on the board.

Kent keeps Cam's chemicals carefully contained.

Percy pointed his pencil purposefully.

**Brooke makes bookmarks.**

Three slick, quick librarians stack
three books on slick, quick poems.

**Lester learns the lesser lesson.**

Sherman surely
subtracts slowly.

328 + 811 = ?????

**Some sums sometimes stump Sam.**

Stella studied states studiously.

School has rules.
Rules are for school.

Allen balances stacks
of valentines.

**Collin collects stickers for Stacey.**

Perfect piles of purple
pencil shavings.

**Hector hangs honeycomb hearts.**

Nancy needed nine
new notebooks.

Raoul cools
on the
school pool
stool.

Knights write right
through the night.

Quinn quickly qualified
the quiz questions.

Sid seldom sees
Sal at school.

**Errol races to erase his errors.**

Pass the purple
paint pot, please.

**Math matters to Matthew.**

Wally wrote rhymes.

**Duke's desk is next to
Luke's and Rex's desks.**

# Under the Sea

Freda feeds the fish fresh food.

"Swim, Stan, swim," sang Sam.

Walruses wipe windows
with white wrinkled rags.

**Sandy's shell socks seem so small.**

**Selfish shellfish.**

Low tide—slow, wide.
Waves collide.

**The crab crawled quickly.**

**During dinner, dolphins eat fish.**

Silvery fish scales
shimmer and shine.

**Finny, Fanny, and Frannie.**

A wave worries a gathering
group of guppies.

**Fish flop freely.**

Firefighter Fred
fetched fresh fish.

**Lobsters sob sloppily.**

**A flabby flounder fouled Flanders's fishing feast.**

Nine white narwhals whistled wildly in the water.

**Conch munch crunchy algae.**

# Six slippery seals swim in the sea.

Sawyer will swim after
Steph and Seth surf.

# Eels feel real eerie!

Baby barracudas
slurp blueberries.

Will's
whale
wears
wool.

The quick, silver squid squealed at the quick quiz.

Orcas orchestrate organized outings.

Is warm water wetter than regular water?

Mark looks for dark, arctic sharks.

Captain Curdie captures
cream-colored crabs.

Look at all the coral colors, Carol!

Manny made many
an anemone enemy.

Floyd found
a fish before
Finn found
a fish.

**Jada drew juggling jellyfish.**

**Wally watched whales wrestle.**

When Sam Sim swims,
he wins.

**Little ripples riffled past.**

**Shining seashells by the sea.**

Bria brought bright
beach blankets.

**Undersea school submarine.**

Squids squirt
sticky substances.

**Six sharp, smart sharks.**

Porpoises parading
in purple pajamas.

**Maureen loves marine life.**

Nowhere are narwhals.

Willy's wet suit whips
over the wave.

Freshly fixed flying fish.

I land only on a lonely island.

Nick's fishnet needs fresh netting.

"The seething sea has ceaseth," said Caesar.

Four flat fish slap fins.

A silly salmon swam in silly salmon school.

**Six shiny sharks shared shortbread.**

Terry took Perry's teal terry cloth towel.

**Rubber boat floating in a moat.**

Bob bobbed the bobber
in the bright blue sea.

**Deepak plucked a ton of plankton.**

Shawna and Shea
shared sunscreen.

Sharika shrieks at the scary shark.

Dolphins golf in fringed scarves.

Alex asks a lot of Allison the axolotl.

When whales swirl,
seaweed whirls.

Sally always shares sunscreen.

**Three sea stars sell sunflowers!**

What kind of noise annoys an oyster?

**Sasha shivered as
she saw sharks.**

**Octopuses
occupy an
octagon in
October.**

Can canned clams
can clams?

Blobfish balance
blobby balloons.

**Porpoises have purposes,
supposedly.**

Slimy, sticky squid
swim south!

**We flow under wonderful flounder.**

These three free reef
fish fish free.

**Malek looks mostly for mollusks.**

Walter whistled wildly
in the water.

See
seahorses
horse
around the
seas.

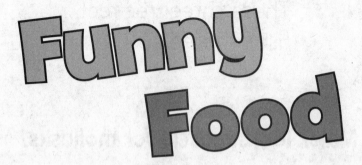

# Funny Food

Chop shops stack chops.

In May, Mayor Mabel
makes maple mayo.

Seven lemon lollipops.

Cam scanned canned ham.

A sweet treat in
the summer heat!

Garry carries cranberries.

**Three slices of cheese pizza, please!**

Chester chose a cheap
chop suey shop.

**Delilah dillydallied at the deli.**

Mama mixed mulberry
muffins on Monday.

**Skylar sliced celery skillfully.**

Barney and Barbara Barber
barbecue burnt bread.

**Crisp crust crackles.**

**Barney the bear ate buttered biscuits and bananas for brunch.**

Golly! Gabby grates grapes for Gabe.

Fried fresh fish, fish fried fresh, fish fresh fried, fresh fried fish.

# Youth yearn for yogurt yearly.

Foolish Freddie fried
fragrant fish for Thursday.

## Can Pam pick pecans?

Sam sings silly songs
while sipping super soup.

## Shelley's shrimp shell soup.

Yolanda's yummy yogurt.

Bridget's blueberry bucket is bigger than Brock's blueberry bucket.

**Crisscrossed pecan piecrust.**

The harried hiker helped
heat the honeyed ham.

**Pooka picks purple peanuts.**

Charles chewed cheese
and Richard chewed gum.

King
Cauliflower.

**Jolly Jeri jars jelly in July.**

Lovely lemony lozenges.

Barry's blueberry baklava beat Bob's blackberry bake at the bake-off.

**The yolk broke while I yodeled.**

Are you all right
with white rice?

**Miss Smith's fish-sauce shop.**

Persimmon's not a
synonym for cinnamon.

**A cupcake cook
in a cupcake
cook's cap cooks
cupcakes.**

**Friendly Frank flips fine flapjacks.**

## Mary made marmalade.

Papa pours a proper cup of coffee from a proper copper coffeepot.

**I see icy ice cream.**

Spencer's spoon makes
prunes palatable.

**Peggy peppered Pedro's pasta.**

Frank's friend Fred found
few fixings for fresh fruit.

Paco
packed
a tasty
taco.

**Musical mules melt marshmallows.**

Flatter pancake batter.

Little lady Lily Lizard licked a lollipop.

Frisco fish fry.

**Will really wanted red raspberries.**

Pecan pie is perfect
for a party.

**Six chickpeas, please!**

Hungry Henry hugs
his hamburger.

**What a treat to eat with Pete!**

The bottom of the butter
bucket is the buttered
bucket bottom.

**Paul picked a particular pickle.**

Picky Pinky picked a pancake.

Matthew made muffins
more milky by mixing
marshmallows.

**Cotton candy can be crunchy.**

Mary and Molly made Mother
mulberry marmalade.

**Crisp crusts crackle crunchily.**

Lilly licked a large
lemon-lime lollipop.

Chloe chose
cheddar
cheese.

**Bruno brings berries.**

Polly pops popcorn in pots.

Petra's pretty
parfait is perfect!

Chill, shake, serve.

**Slush flavor.**

Candace craves
crunchy candy.

**Shane shared sushi with Suzy.**

Charlie chooses
cheese and cherries.

**Top shops stock top chopsticks.**

Frank fried fresh frankfurters
for forty minutes.

Pete's pop, Pete Peters, pops Pete's brand of popcorn.

Chocolate chips on sailing ships.

Supposed to be pistachio.

Try tasting turkey while twirling.

**Fred finds fruit fun.**

A chapped chap chopped chips.

**Three slices of
pumpkin pie, please!**

**Mismatched
Mitch makes
mush.**

Fred fried french fries
for free!

Much mashed mushrooms.

Cassie asked Ashton
for cashews.

Baby Billy buys burritos.

**Arial ate eight apples.**

Mark's mom makes many marvelous mango muffins.

**Bison biting burritos.**

Silly shoofly pie fans sell chilly shoofly pie pans.

**Charlie chooses a cold cup.**

Fred found french fries fresh from France fit for fifty-five families.

Garden Giggles

Reggie juggles every veggie.

"Grow," cheers Gretchen.

Granny grabbed garlic
from Grampy's garden.

# Green grass grows great grapes.

Philip filled his baggage carriage with cabbage.

**Please plant peas!**

**Leif's three trees lose leaves.**

Sparrows splish-splash
in the birdbath.

**Rick rakes recklessly.**

Lilacs lack the flecks
of phlox and flax.

Cacti can't
fuss much.

Twelve tulips and a trowel.

Parker picked a prickly plant.

Seed after seed grows
into garden greens.

Gerald gathers gourds gladly.

**Really red wagon.**

Which witch watched while
Willy washed watermelons?

**"Dig deeper!" demands Derek.**

We weed Wednesdays
when Wendy weeds.

Follow Barry's
flower-barrow!

**Big blossoms bloom bit by bit.**

No one can beat
Beth's sweet beets.

**I envy Ivy's ivy.**

Pines pine.

**Graham grew green grapes.**

**Perfect pink petunias.**

Whose hoe hoes
whose whole holes?

**The thistle's thorns.**

Spencer finishes
mulching his spinach.

**Carrie carts carrots in a carryall.**

Corinne counted loads
of crows in the corn rows.

**Reap ripe pears repeatedly.**

No gnome ever knows which dish to pick.

Lucy let us toss the lettuce.

He heard Herb's
herbs earn awards.

Daisies dazzle Zadie.

**Parker planted plenty of peas.**

Vinnie's vines twine
on Tracey's trellis.

**I raise irises irregularly.**

We eat wheat weekly.

**Bruce prunes spruce.**

The tree roots reached
right round the rock.

**Jo's hose flows slowly.**

**Leo loves lovely lemon leaves.**

## Let Violet's violet violets thrive!

Wren wheels a really
rusty wheelbarrow.

**Grow Greek grapes.**

# Shout about spring sprouts!

Dinesh dines on
dishes of radishes.

## Sun-showers drench sunflowers.

She served superb
herbs for supper.

Pick the plumpest pumpkin!

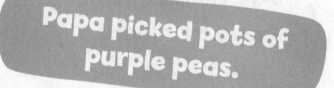
**Papa picked pots of purple peas.**

Grazers mow mostly low grasses.

Plump pumpkins
plopped on the pencil.

**Colleen collects cool collards.**

Two trowels wiped
with one foul towel.

**Should Shaquille shun zucchini?**

Gunther gathers green
beans in his blue jeans.

**Ambrose grows rows and
rows of roses for Rosa.**

Forrest harvests four
flourishing flowers.

**Padma may plant peapods.**

Ripe red radishes
are ready.

**Cover clover cleverly.**

It's time to pick
Tim's thyme.

**Flo found fresh flowers.**

Gerard guards
Garth's garden.

Daphne
dillydallies
by the
daffodils.

Melanie wishes for watermelon slices.

Nine fine veggies on the vine this time!

All hail Kyle's kale!

Pete pickled a pint of peas.

Wild weeds wind in the wind.

Beautiful butterflies flutter by.

Tom grows too many tomatoes.

# Daffy Dinosaurs

Finn found a fantastically frightening fossil.

I dunno—but a dino might!

It's an error to mess with the Mesozoic era!

**T. rex tripped twice.**

*Stegosaurus* stagger sourly.

Pterodactyls tell tall
tall tales of terrible-tasting
tongue twisters.

**Maya swore she saw a *Maiasaura*.**

Sarah swiftly searched
for *Sarahsaurus*.

**T. rex tried trike tricks twice.**

Spooky *Stegosaurus*
spikes surprised Shira.

*Brontosaurus*
basketball
was a bust.

Toss these three hoops on *Triceratops*'s horns.

**Mastodons don't like pasta, Dawn!**

The paleontologist proposed posing proudly in the picture.

**Mister Don misted down the mastodon.**

**True *Troodon* do trod on.**

Neighbor Ruth—drat!—
let loose a sabertooth cat!

***Spinosaurus*, spin for us!**

Dr. Docker determinedly
digs for dinosaur fossils.

THE VALLEY OF EXTINCTVILLE

Jess asks, "Is Jurassic extinct?"

This *T. rex* is perplexed.

'Twas Tara a *Tawa*?

"Not dino—reptile!"
Pterodactyls deny.

Hello, sir! Capture a *Velociraptor*!

**Jurassic 'saurs have spiky jaws.**

Dozing, snoring dinosaurs
do snooze snugly.

*T. rex* **tried trick-or-treating.**

Dina knows no dinos
play dominoes.

**"Please!" paleontologists pleaded.**

Remember the massive
mammoth's mammoth
mouth!

161

**Might dinos dine on dynamite?**

*T. rex* ate eight sticks.

The paleontologist's experiment exceeded expectations.

# Are ichthyosaurs sickly and sore?

Flossie found fifteen
fossils and Fred found five.

## Phoebe possesses feeble fossils.

Shirley, I'm certain that
*Stegosaurus* saw us.

**Try Sara's top
*Triceratops* pie!**

**Pterodactyls are terrible typists.**

Take a trek in *T. rex's* tracks.

Shantelle serendipitously saw *Serendipaceratops*.

*Gryponyx* grip on bricks.

The slanted *Saltasaurus* sign is still sideways!

**This is a** *T. rex's* X-ray.

Shawn was shown unknown dino bones.

**Point to a Bronto on tiptoe— pronto!**

**T. rex imprints ten-foot footprints.**

**Russ bragged he saw four *Brachiosaurus*.**

Celia swears her *Allosaurus* says sorry.

**Axel lost a colossal fossil in a castle.**

Actually, ask Anna, the *Ankylosaurus*.

**Allow *Allosaurus* to sing in the chorus!**

*Corythosaurus*, a Cretaceous creature, carried a crest.

**The thin *Triceratops* turned toward two trees.**

Brave *Brontosaurus* babies break branches.

Dazzling dinosaurs dance delightedly.

Nick's neck knotted noticeably.

Just try stopping a shopping *Triceratops*!

A pterodactyl trio perched precariously on treetops.

**Twelve tyrannosaurs twirled twelve twigs.**

One raucous *Wannanosaurus*,
Two Triassic *Tawa*,
Three tricky *Troodon*,
Four free *Fabrosaurus*,
Five irritating *Irritator*,
Six sneaky *Spinosaurus*,
Seven conniving *Vulcanodon*,
Eight great *Gryponyx*,
Nine nice *Nanotyrannus*, and
Ten thirteen-ton *Triceratops*.

Angelo admires the Ankylosaurus.

# Space Sillies

**Ricky Ridley rides a rocket.**

**Eight aliens ate eighty almonds.**

Chaz chews chocolate
chips on spaceships.

**Shining, shimmering, silver stars.**

Nelly named ninety-nine nebulae.

Marcy shot to Mars,
shouting, "Shooting stars!"

Alexis explores extra galaxies.

**What worlds swirl above Earth?**

Spencer swiftly spun
the space station.

**Carlos cruised across the cosmos.**

The moon's magnificence
moved Maggie.

**In outer space spin great galaxies.**

Lana and Luna had
lunch before launch.

**Did you say *meteor,
meatier,* or *meat-eater?***

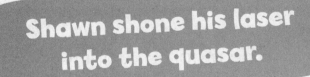

**Shawn shone his laser into the quasar.**

The rover's rickety red wheels worked.

The shy guy says *bye* before he flies in the sky.

## Stella studied stars studiously.

The third grader stayed at the greater crater later.

## Robbie rode a ruby rocket.

A faster asteroid destroyed a speedier meteoroid.

Stan's space socks seem so small.

A one-eyed alien wonders, "Why, Allen?"

Sam sold Susie seven spaceships.

Come comment on the comet, Ahmet!

**Miki likes the Milky Way.**

Eight astronauts ate
eighty cashew nuts.

**Matt most fears the atmosphere.**

Plant plantains on all
the planets, plus Pluto.

**Spaniels respect
space sports.**

**Space snacks mess face masks.**

**Gravy defies gravity!**

Cosmo knows the most about the cosmos.

**Reese's rocket really rocks!**

# Numerous humorous universes!

Martians march through
Mars marshes.

## Sol and Lara are solar scholars.

The lunar rover rove
over the moon sooner.

## He clips eclipse clips.

The farther from Earth we go,
the further of Earth we know.

## Lina tracks lunar ticks.

**Tara's teal telescope tracks far stars.**

## The spaceship tips sideways.

Stacey's spaceship started,
then stopped.

**Shane stares at shining stars.**

Deb hulas in the
February nebula.

**All but Norbert went into orbit.**

Meryl cooks her
curry on Mercury.

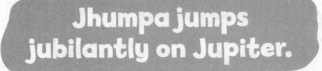
**Jhumpa jumps
jubilantly on Jupiter.**

Uniformed unicorns united in the universe? Unique!

Are Mars moons marshy?

Shep kept in step on Neptune.

**Hugh ran us around Uranus.**

Deep space speeds
Pete's pace.

**Rita readied the wrong rocket.**

What is the girth
of Earth worth?

**Asif spots lots of ocelots in outer space.**

My sole sister set her solar system on this stem.

Saddle a satellite lightly!

It's an asteroid disaster, Roy!

**Silly stars shoot slowly down.**

Rumor of lunar humor?

**Venus is very near us.**

Sue's spacesuit suits Sue.

**An alien alone.**

A stern tern sat on Saturn.

Gravity graffiti.

Janet's planet is made of granite.

The launch is after lunch.

**Rudra's rocket's rudder wobbles.**

Aurora borealis rarely bores Alice.

Brewster blasts his booster's thrusters.

# Creepy-Crawly Chuckles

Seventeen slimy salamanders solemnly slurped several silver seaweed smoothies.

**Careless lazy scaly snakes.**

Itchy inchworms itch
worse after inching.

**My mom met Marvin, my moth.**

Quick cockroaches crawl
quietly.

Five flies fry five fries.

**Ladybugs licked lollipops.**

Big Billy Bee buzzes
by Benny Beetle.

**Frogs favor fables.**

*Swish!* Three pesky
mosquitoes scattered.

**Few free fruit flies fly from flames.**

Legless lizards, like some
skinks, slither skillfully
like snakes.

Twenty-two tired toads tied twine.

Bog frogs flick at fleas
and flies that fly and flee.

Andy asked Aunt Annie all about ants.

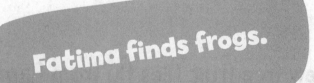
Fatima finds frogs.

**Mud bug.**

One blue bug bled black.
One black bug bled blue.

**Snake sit-ups sound silly.**

Leaping lemon leopard
lizards love large leaves.

The pale snail hauls a
whale pail.

**A cheerful chameleon chuckles.**

Five fat fleas found flea food.

Three tricky turtles
tripped twelve times.

**Lizards leisurely loitered.**

Which woolly worm will
win the winter race?

**Four flying frogs flip-flop festively.**

Five frantic frogs fled
from fifty fierce fishes.

Blake the
snake
bakes
a snack
cake.

**The worm wriggled right.**

That fly flew fast.

Some skinks slither;
some lizards slink.

Six sizzling snakes slurp salsa.

**French flies land on french fries.**

The quick cricket
wove crooked quilts.

**The slug shrugs sluggishly.**

Spiders spin wide,
webbed spirals.

**Geckos gallop gracefully.**

On Sunday, several sneaky
salamanders escaped.

**Big bugs hug on a rag rug.**

Crocodiles cook crooked cookies.

Six sickly silky snakes
slithered silently.

**Super slow snails smell soup.**

Three tree frog families
float freely for fun.

**Frank finds five frogs.**

Slippery silver snakes
sneakily snuck away.

**Sadie spied a spider beside her.**

**Six slow snails slid silently.**

A snake! It shakes! A rattlesnake!

Felicia and Freddy
find frogs on Friday.

# That's how quick Quick Cricket is.

While weevils wearily wave,
wasps wistfully weave.

## Beetle Bug's bigger brother.

Frankie's fabulous frog
ate frozen fly fondue.

**Five firefly friends find flying fun.**

Bea keeps a key in the
beekeeper's tree.

Green geckos gawk.

Mites might meet to
knit mats for gnats.

**The glum grub grew glummer.**

Talented tarantulas
taught tennis.

**Big bats bite bitter berries.**

Eleven earwigs
live in Elvira's elm.

**The groggy grasshopper
gargled.**

## Lucy and Lilly Ladybug bug Billy Bee.

**Aunt Aria rants about ants.**

Three tiny tarantulas
tried tangerines.

**Pythons pick piles of pecans.**

Seeing six spiders,
Sam screamed.

**Mosquitoes make messes.**

Four fat frogs flying past fast.

Tom Turtle took the top
title in the time trial.

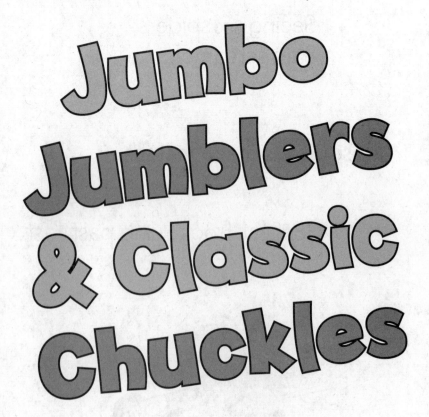

# Jumbo Jumblers & Classic Chuckles

Fuzzy Wuzzy was a bear.
Fuzzy Wuzzy had no hair.
Fuzzy Wuzzy wasn't very fuzzy, was he?

A box of biscuits, a box of mixed biscuits, and a biscuit mixer.

Peter Piper picked a peck of Pickled peppers. A peck of Pickled peppers Peter Piper Picked. If Peter Piper picked A peck of pickled peppers, Where's the peck of pickled Peppers Peter Piper picked?

**Eleven benevolent elephants.**

Green glasses. Green passes. Green basses.

**Rubber baby buggy bumpers.**

A ton of tongue twisters twist my tongue.

**Pad kid poured curd, pulled cod.**

Kate has a kite and a cat. Kate made a cake for her cat. The cat ate the cake, and Kate flew the kite.

**Girl gargoyle, guy gargoyle.**

A pessimistic pest exists amidst us.

Six sick chicks nick six slick bricks with picks and sticks.

Can you can a can as a canner can can a can?

**A loyal warrior will rarely worry why we rule.**

I thought a thought, but the thought I thought wasn't the thought you thought I thought. If the thought I thought had been the thought I thought, I wouldn't have thought I thought.

The sixth sick sheikh's sixth sheep's sick.

She sells seashells by the seashore.

How much wood could a woodchuck chuck if a woodchuck could chuck wood?

Send toast to ten tense stout saints' ten tall tents.

**If two witches were watching two watches, which witch would watch which watch?**

Ronald Rooster wrecked his really red roadster in Worcester at the Rad Red Roadster Rally.

**Tony taught Timmy to tell tongue twisters.**

I wish to wish the wish you wish to wish, but if you wish the wish the witch wishes, I won't wish the wish you wish to wish.

Brisk brave brigadiers brandished broad bright blades, blunderbusses, and bludgeons— balancing them badly.

Pick a partner and practice passing. If you pass proficiently, perhaps you'll play professionally.

Imagine an imaginary menagerie manager managing an imaginary menagerie.

Mares eat oats and does eat oats, but little lambs eat ivy. A kid'll eat ivy, too, wouldn't ewe?

A tree toad loved a she-toad
Who lived up in a tree. He was
A two-toed tree toad, but a
Three-toed toad was she. The
Two-toed tree toad tried to
Win the three-toed she-toad's
Heart, for the two-toed tree
Toad loved the ground that the
Three-toed tree toad trod. But
The two-toed tree toad tried
In vain. He couldn't please her
Whim. From her tree-toed bower,
With her three-toed power, the
She-toad vetoed him.

Toothpaste, moose paste.
Moose paste, toothpaste.
Moose toothpaste,
toothmoose paste.
Toothpaste moose paste.

I would if I could, and if I couldn't, how could I? You couldn't, unless you could, could you?

Betty Botter had some butter.
"But," she said, "this butter's
Bitter. If I bake this bitter
Butter, it would make my
Batter bitter. But a bit of
Better butter, that would
Make my batter better."
So she bought a bit of butter—
Better than her bitter butter—
And she baked it in her batter
And the batter was not bitter.
So 'twas better Betty Botter
Bought a bit of better butter.

**People on a picnic pick pickled peppers. How many pickled peppers do picnicking people pick?**

To begin to toboggan, first
Buy a toboggan, but don't
Buy too big a toboggan. Too
Big a toboggan is too big a
Toboggan to buy to begin
To toboggan.

Rory the warrior and Roger the worrier were reared in a rural area.

Luke Luck likes lakes.
Luke's duck likes lakes.
Luke Luck licks lakes.
Luck's duck licks lakes.
Duck takes licks in lakes Luke
Luck likes. Luke Luck takes
licks in lakes duck likes.

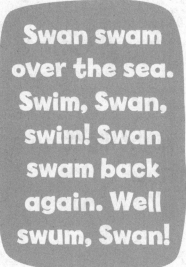

Swan swam over the sea. Swim, Swan, swim! Swan swam back again. Well swum, Swan!

If you must cross a coarse, cross cow across a crowded cow crossing, cross the cross, coarse cow across the crowded cow crossing carefully.

No need to light a night-light on a light night like tonight.

The thirty-three thieves thought that they thrilled the throne throughout Thursday.

Mr. See owned a saw.
And Mr. Soar owned a seesaw.
Now See's saw sawed Soar's
Seesaw before Soar saw See,
Which made Soar sore.
Had Soar seen See's saw
Before See sawed Soar's
Seesaw, See's saw would not
Have sawed Soar's seesaw.

I can think of six thin things and of six thick things, too.

I bought a batch of baking Powder and baked a batch Of biscuits. I brought a big Basket of biscuits back to the Bakery and baked a basket Of big biscuits. Then I took The big basket of biscuits and The basket of big biscuits and Mixed the big biscuits with the Basket of biscuits that was Next to the big basket and Put a batch of biscuits from The basket into a box. Then I Took the big basket of biscuits And the biscuit mixer and the Biscuit basket and brought To the bakery the basket Of biscuits and the box of Mixed biscuits and the biscuit Mixer and took the biscuit Mixer home.

One-one was a racehorse.
Two-two was one, too.
One-one won one race.
Two-two won one, too.

A skunk sat on a stump. The skunk thunk the stump stunk. The stump thunk the skunk stunk. Who stunk? The skunk or the stump?

*Como como poco coco,*
*poco coco compro.*
(Spanish for: "Because I eat very little
coconut, I buy very little coconut.")

Silly Sally swiftly shooed seven silly sheep. The seven silly sheep Silly Sally shooed shilly-shallied south. These sheep shouldn't sleep in a shack; sheep should sleep in a shed.

A tutor who tooted the flute tried to tutor two tooters to toot. Said the two to the tutor, "Is it harder to toot or to tutor two tooters to toot?"

There was a fisherman named Fisher who fished for some fish in a fissure. 'Til a fish with a grin pulled the fisherman in. Now they're fishing the fissure for Fisher.

# Household Humor

Kevin cleaned quickly.

Sheila shined her sister's silver.

Down in the deep, damp, dark, dank den.

Queenie can't quit quilting her question-mark quilt.

The green glass gleamed.

Give Mr. Snipe's wife's butter knife a swipe.

# Dust dust from dawn 'til dusk!

Mother's other daughter ought to be her older daughter.

## Kitchen curtains, kitchen cushions.

Plaid pleated pants.

Three clocks: one ticktocks, two tocktick.

Stephanie stares there on the stairs.

Buy three, get three free!

The tall straw broom stands in the middle of the room.

# Look! Kelly's lucky nickels.

The lad's granddad was the dad when the lad's dad was a lad.

## Clara cleaned the cluttered cupboard.

Bianca's blush brush broke.

Bess dressed in her best dress.

Luke's loose tooth wriggled free.

Chloe closes her clothes closet.

Shauna showed Cheri
Sondra's shoes.

Do not slouch on our new couch.

Velma viewed a vibrant vest.

Funny Frank fell
on the floor Friday.

Burt bought boots.

Perched on the porch,
Porsha purrs perfectly.

See Shawn's shoe shelf.

Audrey laid her laundry
on the lawn to dry.

The faucet flows forcefully.

Ned said he rides his sled in bed.

Shut the shutters utterly tight.

Oksana owns some awesome socks.

This is the sixth sister.

Was Sara so sure she saw Sophie's shoes on the sofa?

**Mister Shuster missed his sister.**

Preshrunk silk shirts.

Sawyer squeezes squishy squirting paste.

Zak's vacuum vroom-vrooms across the room.

Aluminum linoleum.

When the wind blows,
lower the windows.

Soak the silk skirt in the short sink.

**Denise's niece is in the nice den.**

Nervous knights
never knock noisily.

**Shoe-shining shiners shine shoes.**

Which switch switches off
the kitchen dishwasher?

**Queen Corrina collects quills.**

Long slim fingers fiddle
little fiddlesticks.

**Chou chose those shoes.**

## The clock-stopper stopped stopping clocks.

Sam saw six shiny silver spoons.

Sophie snaps a selfie
with her silver cellphone.

# Jack's knapsack strap snapped.

A fly and flea flew through
a flaw in the flue.

## Thirty-six thick silk threads.

Four furious friends fought
for the phone.

PULL

Owen's
door won't
open.

Tosha washes thirty dirty dishes.

Chris cooked crunchy crepes.

Blanca bleached the black beach blanket.

Nick is a pretty persnickety picnicker.

**Claire's clean clock clangs.**

Put a minimum of cinnamon
in the aluminum pan.

**Gale's great glass globe
glows green.**

Never scrub the tub
with a tuba, Bubba!

**Seize the shears and
scissors, Caesar!**

Six shined shoes certainly
should shine.

# Ticklish Travel

**Hawaii hello: "Aloha!"**

**Kansas City's candy shops.**

Which wristwatch is
a Swiss wristwatch?

243

**Never annoy a Nevada otter in the water!**

Gus goes by Blue Goose bus.

I'd have hoed Idaho if Ida
hadn't hoed Idaho wholly.

# Do drop in at the Dewdrop Inn.

Mina sips a mini soda
sold in Minnesota.

## Missy missed Mist Mountain.

Gorgeous George soars
over Georgia's gorges.

Ally's llama
slumbers in
Alabama.

**Don't desert desserts
in the desert.**

I know the one way to Iowa.

Stan stuffs more stuff in
his stuffed suitcase.

# Nick's nephew flees Phoenix.

Marshall marched in marshes with Marcia.

# Ohio has only one lonely *i*.

Miss Moss asks Missy to make a map of Mississippi.

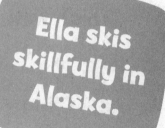

Ella skis skillfully in Alaska.

Fishy singers sang high in Shanghai.

Which way will Wanda wander?

My, oh, my, Ma—my
Omaha home!

Siri surely misses Missouri.

**Connie treks to Connecticut.**

Theo took three
trips to the treetops.

**Denny never dines in Denver.**

Cat catches creative
children camping.

**Which witch hitched to Wichita?**

Jerry needs a new
New Jersey jersey.

**You tore your Utah tutu!**

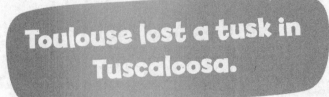

Toulouse lost a tusk in Tuscaloosa.

Fern the fairy flew to the prairie.

Kent caught a tricky Kentucky turkey.

**Maintain every Vermont mountain.**

Sharlene's choo-choo
chugs to Charleston.

**Mae names mainly Maine mares.**

Was Connie wishing
she was in Wisconsin?

**Murray lands merrily
in Maryland.**

Bess steps to the top step at the bus stop, as the bus stops at the best spot.

Flo flew from Florida.

Riley rides the roads after Rose rides.

**Louise and Anna leave Louisiana.**

Joyce enjoys nine
noisy toys from Illinois.

**Intrepid tricksters trekked
to Texas.**

Rhonda rode idly around
Rhode Island.

Tell a lassie
to sail to
Tallahassee.

253

Koalas lack coats in the Dakotas.

Mitch again gains much in Michigan.

Holly would wonder where Hollywood was.

Why are women roaming Wyoming?

**Dash down to Detroit's dock.**

The very best saw ever I saw
to saw was the saw I saw in
Arkansas.

**Della wore Delaware warrior wear.**

Albuquerque quickly
makes Albie quirky.

**Riley rarely wrote from Raleigh.**

You know New York, you need
New York, you know you need
unique New York.

**Train tracks take strange trails.**

**Perry pared pairs of Paris pears.**

Has Rory been sore
again in Oregon?

**Yoko took a yo-yo to Tokyo.**

**Can Ada lease Canada geese?**

Wayne went to Wales
to watch walruses.

**I wish for an Irish wristwatch.**

Scott's scooter stopped
in Scottsdale.

**Greece greets geese graciously.**

Randy roamed around
Rome randomly.

Stan's stuff is stuffed in Stan's tan suitcase.

Fully fill a Philadelphia deli daily.

June knows you know Juneau.

**Glenn plates grains in Great Plains.**

Two timid toads tried to trot to Trenton.

**Lively Olivia lives in lovely Bolivia.**

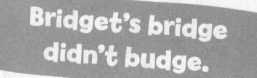

Bridget's bridge didn't budge.

# Weather Whimsy

**Snowstorms, sandstorms, and cyclones, too.**

**Frozen fuzzy feet.**

So much snow fell that
Sue fell in the snow.

Clown clouds crowd around.

Sleet hits the street.

**Sweet shiny sunrise.**

Summer's sizzle fizzles
after a drizzle.

I see icy icicles.

"My yellow umbrella fell!"
the fellow yelled.

Ren wore red rain boots.

The twisting tornado
turned toward two trees.

What do
dragons
do when
raindrops
are due?

**Mitch catches thick flakes in his catcher's mitt.**

Shovel snow slowly.

Silly snowmen make
chilly children smile.

**The sun shines on the shop signs.**

When winter went to one
tree, every tree went wintry.

**Wendy wearies of wet weather.**

Reina's red rain boots are
delightful on damp days.

Loud
lightning
frightens
Flora.

**Leave the leaf leaping to Levi.**

Hari can hurry in a hurricane.

They saw the thaw
they thought they saw.

"It's spring!" sang Sean.

**We'll all have a ball in fall.**

A wily worm will wiggle
while he's warm.

**Snow showers show slowly.**

Wendy went wading on
a windy Wednesday.

**Foggy bogs bother soggy frogs.**

Whether Heather weathers
the weather, the weather will
weather Heather.

**Windy days daze Wendy.**

**Desi dreads the dry desert.**

Frozen flecks of frosty
flakes fly freely.

**Feet slip on slick sleet.**

The loud, proud cloud
bowed to the crowd.

**Floyd avoids floods.**

Cindy wears a sweater
in windy weather.

The tornado
tore through
Toronto.

Umberto's under the weather
under his umbrella.

Some sun sometimes.

Downpours pour down
drain spouts.

Fez finds his fox in the fog.

**Hail hailed on Hal's hill.**

Short squalls scare
small squirrels.

**Susan chooses freezing season.**

Tuesday, a twister
swished through.

**Gutters gush as rain rushes.**

Lesser leather never
weathered wetter weather
better.

**Many poodles play in muddy puddles.**

Warren rathers warmer weather.

Our blue boat is better
in this weather.

# A gust blows Augusta's bows.

Lazy lizards lie in
freezing blizzards.

## The weather will wither the wreath.

Fifi and her friends
aren't afraid of frost.

No nose knows
snow like a
snowman's
nose knows.

## Willy wanted warm water while washing windows on Wednesday.

Sudden summer thunder.

Norm storms out into the morning storm.

Snow boots, snowsuits.

**Autumn often offers orange hues.**

Sula sulks at stormy
Sunday showers.

**Ice is twice as nice on a hot day.**

It's too hot to heat
the hot dogs.

**Icicles tickle Kiki.**

Whitney had written a
reminder about wearing
mittens.

**Petra Parker picked a purple parka.**

Brisk breezes risk big sneezes.

Sasha sloshes through the slush.

**Wind whips over the water.**

Mr. Whiskers seeks
misty vistas.

**William's hair whips in the wind.**

I see icy ice-skaters.

# Playtime Tee-Hees

Penguin guests in disguise.

Paula picks pink paper.

Tyler took a turn on
Trevor's toboggan.

**Freddy flung festive confetti.**

Broken blue crayon.

Jill and Jack jump
on the jungle gym.

**Shawn draws the short straw.**

Sally steps on stepping stones every seven seconds.

**Toni and Tori tell Terri to twirl.**

Doug double-dog dares Dawn downhill.

**Stan planned a one-handed handstand.**

**Penny paints pink pigs.**

**Brooke broke Renata's piñata.**

Barry blew big
beautiful bubbles.

Buster burst a bazillion balloons.

*Whoosh* whirred the
wheels on Wren's ride.

**Fiery fireworks fly high in the sky.**

Spring makes Spike and
Mike want to bike.

**Gracie
traces with
giant crazy
crayons.**

## The pitcher's pitch missed Mitchell.

**Give gifts gleefully.**

Pepperoni pie is
perfect for a party.

**Color-painted tie-dyed T-shirts.**

Cal could canoe if Cam came, too.

The Scorpions' score
ties with the Titans'.

Mimi made many memories.

Ron rolled a round
ball at the race.

Freddy's friends play freeze tag.

Betty and Bob brought
back blue balloons from the
big bazaar.

Yannick yanked a yellow yo-yo.

Sam saw a white kite in flight.

Tim takes Todd's tickets.

# Karen's kick came to Connor.

Young Yardley brought his yarn to yoga.

## Bessie's big brother yelled, "Boo!"

Bart and Brett keep the beat with their feet.

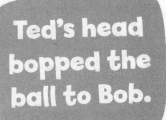

Ted's head bopped the ball to Bob.

"Bigger bubble, better bubble," boasts Blaire.

Pat picked purple presents.

Mitch didn't miss
much of the match.

Piper prepped the party plates.

**Bella blows blue bubbles.**

Blake's bike is bigger,
but Betty's bike is better.

**Carly carted crates of crafts.**

Cam can't decide—swim with
Clyde or slide with Jim?

**Duncan Duck ducks dodgeballs.**

Even when one of Juan's
wheels was wobbly, he still
won!

Would Keith catch
Seth's pass?

Flora floats faster than Farah.

The wretched runner ran
around the rough and
rugged rock.

**Greg's green helmet helps him.**

Silly Sally's sled always slips sideways.

**Keely Klaus's kite soars.**

Cameron's quick wit won him the role.

Tom's cheese cheers his home team.

Patti practiced batting
bigger bubbles.

Mike might like to bike to Spike's.

Mitch might miss the
monster movie.

Parker plays in the park.

**Ronan borrowed Reba's rowboat.**

Judy juggles and jumps
at the gym.

**Rowdy roller-coaster riders.**

Paola owns oodles of
pool noodles.

**Will lets Ron win.**

Gentle Janeen juggled
jumping jelly beans while
jumping over jacks at the
gym.

Regular roller-coaster riders ride right up front.

Purple paper people.

Racing Russell ran on wobbly, rainy rocks.

# Nancy notices Nate next to the net.

Newt and Anita need a new net now!

## Patches picked the purple paint.

Pigs play pinball at pizza palaces.

Colin carries colorful cones.

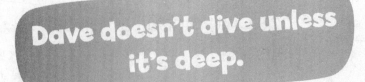

**Dave doesn't dive unless it's deep.**

Schwartz Source for Sports.

Random words make witty rhymes.

Carnes carts crates of crafts.

**Fred from Florida floats freely.**

Scott hopes to hopscotch happily.

**Homer races to home base.**

Brooke bought a bright blue bike.

**Batters better bat better.**

Bobby balanced the ball on his back.

**Tootie wears a turquoise tutu.**

**Brynlee blew up a blue balloon.**

**Skinny ski slope.**

Greg gave Gavin a
green gift.

Jack's backflip flops.

Can Kate climb like Kim can?

Three free throws.

Purple panthers prance
proudly.

Darren dare not toss darts at the heart art.

Esther exercises excitedly.

Children chuckle cheerily.

Dave developed his
dunk with Dale.

Chloe collects clean coins.

Ned needs another nylon net.

Please pass Bo's party
bags fast.

Chris kicked a clean can.

Brent's black brick
box broke.

Patty prints pretty ponies.

Drew dribbles during drills.

Sticky stickers stick swiftly.

# Crazy Construction

Hattie hatched huge house plans.

Drew drilled deep.

Cedar shingles should be shared and saved.

**Does Bill doze by those bulldozers?**

**Nick picks bricks.**

Wheldon welds wells while Wilma welds wheels.

**Low rails need new nails.**

Freddy Flanders fell face-first fixing faucets for friends.

**Shaw sees a saw on the seesaw.**

Pavi put the puffy putty partly on Patty's patio.

Rachel reaches with her roller.

A house had a mouse and the mouse had a house inside.

Some plumbers slumbered while some numbered lumber.

Flimsy framing frustrates Frank.

Rick bought blocks at the Brick Boutique.

One white stone weighs one ton.

Mabel's able to make
a stable maple table.

Havel shovels gravel gravely.

Ceci meant to set
symmetrical cement.

The tall tower towers over the lower tower.

**Damp muck stuck Chuck's dump truck.**

Piper places pipes properly.

Many mulching mowers mulch much more in March.

As big as big can be, but bigger.

**Layla laid logs lengthwise.**

Hannah hammers homemade hammocks.

**Chris can't crush cans.**

Breaking black bricks is backbreaking.

**Bruce loses loose screws.**

The leader later laid down the ladder.

Pine or oak? Pinocchio's nose knows.

Richard's wretched ratchet wrench.

Bright white light fills the large log lodge.

# Tool belts hold two bolts.

Bill builds with thick slick brick blocks.

## Real rock wall.

Sid sets smooth stones side by side.

Hadley had her hard hat at hand.

**Diego dug deeper than Doug did.**

**Max hacks oaks with Jack's ax.**

Seal the ceiling with sparkling spackle.

**Why are wires so wiry?**

**Buck plunked planks in the trunk.**

Jimmy fixes the chinks in the chimney.

**Lay the fat slats flat.**

Todd told Tony to tow the tow truck.

**Celia sells six steel screws.**

Zeke seeks the source of the leaks.

**Blotchy blue prints on the blurry blueprints baffle Biff.**

**Winch the wrench on the ranch.**

Pry the pliers from the pile of fliers.

**Frank's forklift lifts four kits.**

Trevor tried not to trip on the tarp.

**A straw house stays strong.**

Rain ruined the crew's crane.

**Nick's pickax acts pickier than Ricky's.**

**Trust Trudy to transport tools.**

Morty mortars tarry molars.

Fix the bricks with mixed sticks.

**Pavel paves pathways perfectly.**

Will works on the red
rock wall.

**Upper roller, lower roller.**

Blue glue gun, green
glue gun.

**Dex's deck looks wrecked.**

Cassie's castle stands
on sand.

Amusing Music

Too bad tubas can't scuba.

## Max tracks sax facts.

A mellow fellow chose
a yellow cello.

**DJ Duck spins thirty-six tracks.**

**Ruth toots a flat flute.**

Trudy dumped her trumpet on the trampoline.

320

**Joe jams with his banjo band.**

Pippa is a peppier piper than Pepe.

**Hippos hip-hop happily.**

No note is more noticeable than an eighth note.

Maggie's bagpipe makes big music.

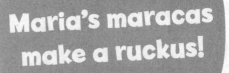
**Maria's maracas make a ruckus!**

**Miguel and Mikayla move to music.**

Woodrow's woodwind's
sticky keys stuck.

**Penelope plays piano perfectly.**

Veronica's harmonica is mistaken for Monica's.

**Thelma sings the theme song.**

Pam's timpani symphony is simply fantastic!

Oh, why did our choir hire a higher singer?

323

**Jody yodels nobly.**

# Magnificent musicianship.

Viola loves her violet violin.

# Mike on a mic mimics Mickey.

Timothy's tin whistle
whistles timidly.

**Bette's baton keeps the beat.**

Gordon records an accordion
encore accordingly.

Rick and Raj really rock!

**Lydia's little fiddle fiddles fittingly.**

## Our chorus chose Doris!

Honey has many harmony memories.

Patrick picks a practical piccolo.

A cymbal is a symbol
of a simple implement.

**Walt waits to waltz with Willa.**

Tom's palms thump on the
tom-toms.

A single
flamingo brings
a bongo or a
banjo.

**His xylophone's style of tone is Kyle's alone.**

**Chaz says his jazz has pizzazz.**

Fifi's fife riffs swiftly.

**Liam's thumb strums in rhythm.**

**Erika likes Eric's lyrics.**

Danika blew a kazoo
at the Kalamazoo zoo!

**Flo's flute toots fluidly.**

Melanie made a medley
of melodies.

**Sally sang simple songs softly.**

Got a great guitar to get a
greater guitar to greet the
greatest guitarist.

**Christine is seen jangling a tangerine tambourine.**

# Tom's trombone booms!

To do a duet, does it
take a duo to do it?

**This is a zither.**

Did Jerry do jingles on
his didgeridoo?

**Poppa's polka woke Rocco.**

Morgan owns an organ
from Oregon.

Baboons
soon tune
their
bassoons.

Lara sang Sarah's long song.

The fair flutist flung fruit.

Papa's opera operates properly.

# Harper's harp has no F sharp!

Octavia's arias have eight octaves.

## Toby obeys our oboe pro.

Click your castanet faster, Chester!

## Shawn's horn warns: it's morning!

Rob raps wrapped in a ripped robe.

Mister Masters is a messy music maestro.

Clarence's clarinet is clearly wet.

Sit the soprano at the piano.

**Jim's chimes chime
at prime time.**

Luckily, Luke likes ukuleles.

**Doug rung the wrong
gong strongly.**

Six sassy saxophones sit.

**Some drums thrum, some
drums hum, some are
humdrum.**

Gab
Grab
Bag

**Frowning clowns show glowing crowns.**

**Quick!** Switch wristwatches.

Wanda wondered where
Wally went.

**Stu stubs his stubby toes.**

Red leather, yellow leather.

The scientist's experiment
exceeded expectations.

**River level.**

"Yikes, Yasmeen!
You and I look alike."

## Thin grippy, thick slippery.

Plymouth sleuths thwart
Luther's slithering.

Harriet's
huge hair
has rare
hues.

Three Y guys in disguise yell, "Surprise!"

Whistle for the thistle sifter.

Scamper quickly!

Robin's ribbed ribbon ripped!

Hearty Harry hurried.

Near an ear, a nearer ear,
a nearly eerie ear.

"Yes! Yes!" says Yvette.

"Throw out nothing!"
thought Thrifty Teddy.

Click, clap, pluck.

Aaron's parents, presently
present, apparently present
presents.

**The globby glob gobbled.**

Tim's time topped Tom's time.

Washington wished for
white whiskers.

**Three short sword sheaths.**

Theo thought that
through thoroughly.

**One hundred hungry hunters.**

Ah, shucks! Six stick
shifts stuck shut!

Lawrence lounged on the
long lawn lounge.

**Both boys bought polka-dot bows.**

## The rugged rascal rudely ran.

The squire squashed the queen's wreaths.

**Vivien's vivid vests vex Vixen.**

Sam's shop stocks
short spotted socks.

**Please pay promptly.**

Thin kings swing thinking of
sparkling rings.

**Double bubble blowers blow doubly big bubbles.**

The president proposed posing proudly in the picture.

Slippery silver slippers, please!

Samantha smiles after a single sip.

**Wilma's really weary.**

Willy sent a silly
scent to Millicent.

**Gig whip.**

Tim Smith, the thin
twin tinsmith.

Darla's dollar
bothered her.

Shelly Shane smiles at sales at the Shutter Shop.

**Flash message!**

Wally walks while
Wyatt waves.

# A red leather lump.

Lesser leather never weathered.

## Merl, the rural juror.

Sheera sold soft-soled shoes.

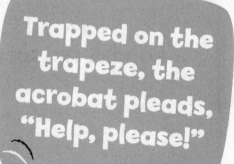

Trapped on the trapeze, the acrobat pleads, "Help, please!"

**Our skater waiter scatters platters.**

Ronda's red rock.

Dust is a disk's worst risk.

Wendy wobbled once.

Yesterday, I yawned wearily.

**Tom told Timmy to talk to Tony.**

Loyal royal lawyer.

**Wanda's wristwatch works!**

Stupid superstition!

**The owner of the Inside Inn was outside his Inside Inn looking inside.**

Swiss wristwatch.

## All alarms alarmed Armand.

Shoe section.

Truly rural.

Twelve twins twirled tree twigs.